LITTLE PLATYPUS

Inspiring | Educating | Creating | Entertaining

Brimming with creative inspiration, how-to projects, and useful information to enrich your everyday life, quarto.com is a favorite destination for those pursuing their interests and passions.

First published in 2022 by QEB Publishing,
an imprint of The Quarto Group.
100 Cummings Center,
Suite 265D Beverly, MA 01915, USA.
T (978) 282-9590 F (978) 283-2742
www.quarto.com

Editorial Assistant: Alice Hobbs
Art Director: Susi Martin
Publisher: Holly Willsher

A CIP record for this book is available from the Library of Congress.

ISBN: 978-0-7112-7418-1

9 8 7 6 5 4 3 2 1

Manufactured in Guangdong, China TT062022

LITTLE PLATYPUS

illustrated by
REBECA PINTOS

ANNA BRETT

Good evening, I'm Little Platypus.
The sun might be setting outside,
but my mommy, my twin brother,
and I are just waking up, ready
to start our day. Let me tell you all
about our small but happy family.

Baby platypuses are called puggles!

We live on the side of a riverbank in eastern Australia. Our home is a burrow with the entrance hidden by overhanging plants.

This helps keep us safe and out of sight
since all three of us are very shy!

7

Our mommy is always telling us how handsome we are! We have webbed feet and a bill like a duck, a body like an otter, and a tail like a beaver.

And do you like my thick, waterproof fur? It's dark brown on top and light brown on my tummy.

My brother and I are heading out of the
burrow for a *swimming lesson*.

I love playing in the river water, especially diving down to the bottom.

I can hold my breath for up to two minutes, but then I have to come back to the surface for air.

Mommy is helping me learn how to use my tail and feet to move faster in the water.

11

All this swimming is making me hungry.

I'm still learning how to hunt for my food.

So for now I'll scoop up a mouthful of gravel and mud from the riverbed and hope there's something tasty in there! The gravel helps me chew because we platypuses don't have any teeth.

Finding food at the bottom of the riverbed in the dark of night is not easy. But Mommy is teaching us about our super sixth sense—electroreception. This is our ability to detect the electric currents made by prey moving in the water.

She shows us how she moves her head from side to side so her bill can sense the currents.

We close our eyes, nose, and ears when diving, so the electroreception sense is essential for finding food.

Time for a rest back in the burrow. Mommy dug our burrow all by herself, using just her claws. It's got a clever design: the entrance is really narrow so only one of us can enter at a time—and it helps squeeze out the water from our fur.

17

17

Let's peek out of the burrow together! Our male neighbor is playing tag through the water with a female.

They are grabbing each other's tails with their bills to show affection! Hopefully this means they will couple up and there might be some new babies arriving soon.

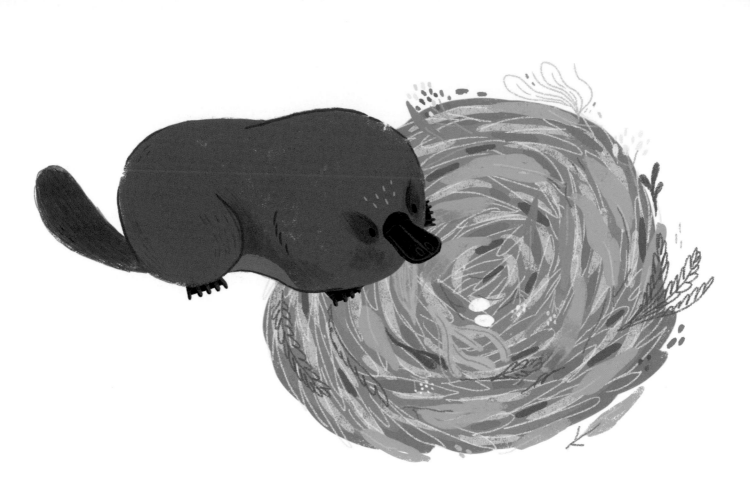

Guess what? We platypuses are mammals, but
the females actually lay small, leathery eggs like
reptiles! Mommy platypuses then curl themselves
around the eggs to keep them safe and warm in the
burrow for ten whole days.

Females lay between one and three eggs.

After ten days of incubation,
platypus eggs are ready to hatch.

I was this small just
four months ago!

Newborn babies are tiny and not ready to leave the burrow yet, so they stay safely hidden inside and lap up the milk that oozes from their mommy's skin.

I'm a male platypus, so I have a spike on my back legs called a spur. It can release poisonous venom, but I'll only use it if I am in danger.

I know that adult males sometimes fight
when it's time to mate with the females.

25

We leave our burrow at night, which means there's less chance predators will be able to spot us. Although we are quick in the water, we are slow and clumsy on land and foxes could easily catch us.

27

Time for a bath before bedtime—it's so much fun to play in this flowing water with my brother.

Mommy uses the little nails under her webbed feet to give our fur a brush as well.

Yawn! It's nearly sunrise so it's time for us
to head back home for some sleep.

Mommy has filled the burrow with wet leaves to keep us cool, just how we like it. We sleep in a chamber at the end of our riverbank burrow.

It's been a busy night of learning for me and my brother—time for a long sleep now. Soon we'll leave Mommy and her burrow and make our own way down the river to find a new area to live in.

32

But for now, our family of three will
enjoy snuggling up together.

FUN FACTS

Thank you for joining me tonight. It was a pleasure to introduce you to my family and show you around our riverside home!

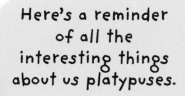

Here's a reminder of all the interesting things about us platypuses.

- Platypus have webbed feet and a bill like a duck, a body like an otter, and a tail like a beaver.

- Platypuses are active at night, meaning they are nocturnal.

- They build burrows in the soft soil of the riverbank.

- Platypuses have a sixth sense—electrolocation. It allows them to detect electric pulses given out by other animals.

- Females lay eggs like a reptile, but produce milk to feed their young like a mammal.

- Males have a venomous spur on their rear legs.

- Platypuses don't have teeth.

- They are excellent swimmers and have webbed feet to help them paddle.

FACT FILE

Average length: 20 in for males, 16 in for females

Average weight: 2.2–5.3 lbs for males, 1.3–3.1 lbs for females

Lifespan: Up to 21 years in the wild

Swimming speed: 3 feet per second

DUCKING AND DIVING

Can you tell which platypus lives in this burrow? Follow the ripples in the water to find out.

a

b

c

Which jigsaw piece completes the picture of this swimming platypus?

CONSERVATION

We know that platypuses are shy creatures and hard to spot in the wild, but declining numbers are now making them even harder to find.

Drought, bushfires, pollution and urban development in Australia have impacted our habitat over the years.

The Royal National Park in Sydney will provide a new home for ten platypuses.

Luckily, people have come up with several conservation methods— ways that humans can improve the outlook for these fascinating creatures.

Platypuses haven't been seen in the Royal National Park, south of Sydney, since the 1970s. But ten lucky platypuses are going to be introduced into a suitable waterway soon! They will be monitored and protected so they can populate more of the park and thrive.

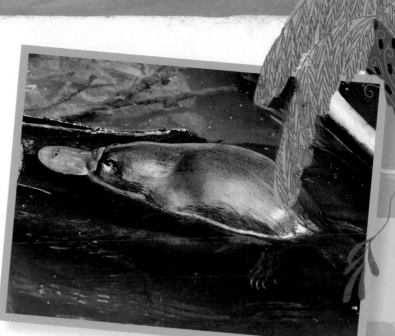

This platypus is having a short rest outside of the burrow.

A platypus climbing out of the water, Atherton Tablelands, Queensland, Australia

People will of course be eager to catch a glimpse of these unique animals, so special walkways and viewing platforms will be set up so they don't disturb the habitat or the platypuses.

LOOKALIKES

Can you spot the five differences between these two platypuses swimming along the river?

The sun is setting and casting shadows. Which shadow matches this young platypus sitting on the riverbank?

PAPER BAG PLATYPUS PUPPET

YOU WILL NEED

- A brown paper bag, rectangle shaped
- Purple, brown, and white cardstock
- Scissors
- School glue
- A black pen

1 Place the flat paper bag on a table with the open end facing down. Fold in the corners of the base of the bag, as shown.

2 Cut out a tail shape from the brown cardstock, like this. Glue to the back of the open end of the paper bag.

3 Cut out four webbed feet from the purple cardstock, and draw five fingers within each of the feet with your black pen. Glue two feet to the bottom corners of the bag, and two halfway up the edges of the bag.

4 Time to add the bill, so cut out this shape, as shown, and glue it over the end of the base of the bag. Use your black pen to add two dots for the nostrils.

YOUR PUPPET IS COMPLETE!

5 Cut out and stick on two white eyes above the bill, then use your black pen to add the pupils.

RESCUE AND RELEASE

Although we are a very shy species, sometimes contact with humans can help us. Here's a story about rescue and rehabilitation that helped seven of my cousins survive.

In December 2019 parts of southeastern Australia were struggling with drought and bushfires. As a fire approached the Tidbinbilla Nature Reserve, outside Canberra, the teams responsible for the wildlife became very

Bushfires are fires that burn and spread quickly across dry bushland, grassland and forests.

worried for the platypuses and other animals that live in the area. They contacted Taronga Zoo in Sydney, asking if they could shelter their platypuses until the danger had passed. The zoo agreed and sent a rescue team out to collect seven platypuses.

They housed them at the zoo but made sure they had their privacy and kept interactions with humans limited, to keep life similar to what they knew.

Once the drought ended and the ponds in the reserve filled with water, the team returned the platypuses back to their home.

A platypus receives a health check at Sydney's Taronga Zoo.

Towels are used to make the platypuses feel warm and safe.

Tracking devices told them that the group are happy and healthy and enjoying safety once again.

Since then a new Platypus Rescue and Rehabilitation Centre has been established at the zoo to help future generations of this animal.

QUIZ

How much do you know about the amazing platypus? Try this quiz and see if you can remember all the unique features of these animals.

The answers are on page 48.

1. A platypus looks like three animals combined. Do you know what they are?

    A. Duck, otter, and beaver

    B. Fish, water vole, and frog

    C. Seal, squirrel, and kangaroo

2. In which country do platypuses live in the wild?

3. True or false: platypuses lay eggs.

4. Platypuses dig their home in the riverbank. What is it called?

5. Platypuses have teeth, true or false?

6. What do baby platypuses drink when they are first born?

7. Are platypuses faster on land or in water?

8. True or false: females have a spur on their legs.

9. How many senses do platypuses have: two, four, or six?

10. True or false: platypuses sleep at night.

ANSWERS

P36-37

P40-41

Picture credits

P34 slowmotiongli / Shutterstock. P35 top: Minden Pictures / Alamy Stock Photo, bottom: blickwinkel / Alamy Stock Photo. P37 Minden Pictures / Alamy Stock Photo. P38 Karen H Black / Shutterstock. P39 top: Greg Wyncoll / Shutterstock, bottom: Laura Romin & Larry Dalton / Alamy Stock Photo. P44 Tracey Nearmy / Stringer / Getty. P45 top: Mark Metcalfe / Stringer / Getty, bottom: The Sydney Morning Herald / Getty. P47 top: Dave Watts / Alamy Stock Photo, P47 bottom: Minden Pictures / Alamy Stock Photo

1. A. Duck, otter, and beaver
2. Australia
3. True
4. A burrow
5. False
6. Milk
7. Faster in water
8. False—it's the males that have spurs
9. Six—sight, hearing, taste, touch, smell and electrolocation
10. False—they hunt at nighttime